Alex Ngumbi

Consumer behavior analysis of Chinese Auto Industry against foreign giant companies

GRIN Verlag

Bibliografische Information der Deutschen Nationalbibliothek:

Die Deutsche Bibliothek verzeichnet diese Publikation in der Deutschen National-bibliografie; detaillierte bibliografische Daten sind im Internet über http://dnb.d-nb.de/ abrufbar.

Imprint:

Copyright © 2012 GRIN Verlag GmbH
Druck und Bindung: Books on Demand GmbH, Norderstedt Germany
ISBN: 978-3-656-55480-6

This book at GRIN:

http://www.grin.com/en/e-book/265539/consumer-behavior-analysis-of-chinese-auto-industry-against-foreign-giant

Consumer behavior analysis of Chinese Auto Industry

against foreign giant companies

Table of contents

1. Introduction

The automotive industry in China is the biggest in the entire world based on the per unit production of this industry back in 2008. The total annual automobile production in China was much more than of Japan, US and the European Union in the year 2009. Around 44.3% of the total automobile production was of the local brands whereas others were manufactured by joint ventures with the foreign producers like Volkswagen, Hyundai, Honda, General Motors, Nissan, Mitsubishi, and Toyota. The home market in China provides a very strong base to the automakers and the economic planners in China are hoping to establish auto companies that are globally competitive (Zhao, 2009).

The automobile industry of China mainly had Soviet origins and the initial 30 years of the nation produced small volumes only. China was found to produce more than 2 million vehicles in 2000. The national automobile industry of China had grown by 21% on an average from the year 2002 to 2007. The production capacity of China was much more than 7 million in 2006 and by 2007; it was producing around 8 million automobiles. In the year 2009, the production was around 13.79 million vehicles out of which 8 million automobiles were passenger cars and around 3.41 million were found to be commercial vehicles. In the year 2010, both the production and sales exceeded 18 million units, which were the highest in the history of automobile industry. In 2009, there were about 62 million registered trucks, vans, buses, and cars in China which is expected to reach 200 million by the year 2020 (Amighini, 2012).

In the year 2010, China was known to be the biggest global exporter of automobiles and the 2nd largest country globally after the United States. China attracted joint ventures and foreign direct investments. Foreign brands played a significant role in affecting the manufacturing and consuming sector of this economy. It helped in providing great diversity in designs, attractive appearance, quality, and choice within the consuming sector. These brands also alleviated the shortfalls in the consumer goods existing bds in a large number of product categories.

This research study aims at making great contribution to the existing literature on country of origin concept from the viewpoint of the Chinese customers. This study will specifically investigate two key points. Firstly, the significance of the manufacturing nation of the product compared to the attributes of the choice of the Chinese consumers and secondly, the relative significance of the country image aspect of the consumer's preference of the foreign goods.

It is important to conduct a systematic investigation regarding the concept of country of origin in the developing countries as it has its effects on the exporters, foreign manufacturers, domestic manufacturers, marketers, and various channel intermediaries wishing or doing business in such countries. It also has its effect on the policy makers and government of the developing nations trying to develop domestic manufacturing competencies during intense competition from the foreign brands and also for the academics that are interested in comprehending the behavior of the consumers in the developing countries (Barbosa, 2010).

2. Background

China is known to be the world's biggest consumer and producer of automobiles even though the behavior of Chinese consumers within this market is not studied adequately. This study will investigate the significance of country image and country of origin for evaluation of the Chinese consumer and their purchase intentions for automobiles. The respondents who were surveyed came from ten of the Chinese cities. A conjoint analysis had been done to determine the significance of the country of origin compared to the other attributes for making preference judgments. Multiple regressions were used for determining the significance of country image in making the purchase decisions. It had been found that brand name and country of origin are equally important and are more important compared to safety, reliability, and price in making product evaluations. In addition, workmanship, reliability, and superior prestige were more significant reasons for the Chinese respondents to prefer foreign automobiles compared to the Chinese brands (Chiu, 2011).

3. Research Question

Is Chinese auto industry surviving despite the growing competition by foreign auto industry brands? Are Chinese consumer behavior perceptions and preferences leaning more towards Chinese companies than that of foreign companies?

4.   Research Aim

The main aim of this research is to examine current situation of Chinese auto industry and the factors which have contributed on the success of immense growth rate of Chinese auto industry confronting sever competition from foreign automobile companies.

5.   Research Objectives

- To study the current Chinese auto industry and the growing competition in the industry

- To evaluate the concept of consumer behaviour and the factors impacting the consumer buying behaviour with respect to auto industry

- To review various literatures and academic published in the context of consumer behaviour and Chinese auto industry

- To study the factors which may hamper the growth of Chinese auto industry as a result of growing foreign giant companies

6.   Literature Review

According to Batra (2009) consumer behavior is all about the study of organizations, groups or individuals and the processes used by them to secure, select and dispose the ideas, experiences, services and products for satisfying the impacts and needs made by such processes on the society and consumers. It helps in comprehending the buyer's decision-making process both in groups and individually. It also helps in studying the individual consumer characteristics like behavioral and demographic variables to understand the wants and desires of people. It also helps in assessing the impact on the consumers from groups like society, reference groups, friends, and family (Batra, 2009).

Studying the behavior of customers depends on the buying behavior of the consumers as they play three different roles of being the buyer, payer, and user. Research studies have proved that it is difficult to foretell consumer's behavior. Consumer retention, one-to-one marketing, customer customization, personalization, and relationship management are also greatly

4

important. Social functions are divided as welfare functions and social choice. Homogeneity, unanimity, monotonicity, anonymity, neutrality, and decisiveness are the key specifications of a social function. Identifying the interactive effect of the alternatives and establishing the logical association with ranks is the most significant feature of social functions (Berkman, 1997).

As per study by Blythe (2008) since the last 40 years, researchers have been studying the effect of country of origin regarding a product on the consumer's choice. Country of origin along with brand name and price are the key extrinsic cues for evaluating consumer products. Country of origin, brand name, and price are those extrinsic cues, which are used in absence of direct experience, or intrinsic cues with regard to a product for inferring attributes that are difficult to evaluate like the product's reliability, performance, and quality. Therefore, a customer might use their perception regarding the country of origin of some unknown brand in order to infer the probable quality or intrinsic attributes of that brand (Blythe, 2008).

A number of studies taken place in the developed nations showed that customers there prefer products of the developed nations compared to the ones from the less-developed nations. They specifically prefer the domestic goods rather than goods imported from other nations. Large number of evidences exist which show that Americans have greater preference for goods made in America rather than foreign goods. However, other findings show that preference for the domestic products varies from nation to nation and is not a universal concept. A hierarchy of nations had been proposed depending on the type of economic development (Loudon, 2001).

According to Wright (2006) products manufactured in nations, which are having a low hierarchy, are of poor quality compared to the goods coming from higher hierarchies. It was also found that Dutch, German, Canadian, and American customers prefer domestic television sets and car radios following the ones belonging to developed nations and lastly the ones in the developing nations. Research studies also showed that the significance of the country of origin differs from nation to nation. American respondents ranked first in preferring their domestic television sets and Germans for preferring car radios.

Consumers are likely to have a preference for the domestic products in nations where consumer ethnocentrism, national pride, and patriotism are quite strong. This preference is quite weak in underdeveloped nations, which are economically not developed. Consumers belonging to the socialist nations of Central and Eastern Europe, which is being transformed into marketing economies, are likely to prefer western products than central (Wright, 2006).

Now it is clear that customers from different nations react differently to the notion of country of origin. It is also seen that the assessments associated with country-of-origin are quite dynamic meaning that economic development of a country improves its country of origin state both abroad and at home. Country of origin, manufacture, assembly, and design create varied effects on evaluation of consumer products. For example, some of the affluent consumers in Hong-Kong do not prefer buying German luxury cars, which have been assembled in China. They seem to prefer the ones that have been assembled in Germany being more expensive. Therefore, such customers react in a favorable manner to Germany, the country of origin and not to China, the manufacturing country (Barbosa, 2010).

The Chinese Automobile Industry

The Chinese automobile industry is the world's largest in context with its production volume and has been growing rapidly since 2008. However, this industry has been seeing growth in China since 1990. The main reason for this growth is the rapid growth of the middle class in China. The foreign manufactures of automobiles entered into strategic alliances along with the local firms with the government of China limiting the ownership to 50% for capitalizing this rapid growth and for acquiring manufacturing at a low cost. The annual production of automobile in China was more than 1 million in the year 1992. Chins had produced more than 2 million automobiles in 2000. There was rapid growth in production since 2000 with 6 million vehicles in 2006 and around 8 million by 2007, 13.8 million by 2009 and 17.2 million by 2010. In 2011, the rate of growth had fallen but still selling 18.5 million new automobiles (Warburton, 2008).

In that year itself, 850,000 automobiles had been exported with Iran, Brazil, and Russia leading the export value. 44.3% of the vehicle production in 2009 was done by the local brands with the rest being manufactured by government owned Chinese companies and joint ventures. It includes BMW, Mercedes, Honda, Hyundai, Mitsubishi, Ford, Toyota, Nissan, General Motors, and Volkswagen.

The leading automobile company of China is General Motors after which is Volkswagen each having a market share of more than 10%. The foreign manufacturers entering joint

6

ventures accounted 70% of the domestically formed automobile market. The all-new government of China planned to make the market share of the domestic manufacturers increase by 50% in 2015. However, the domestic market is still a baby in context with R&D, product features, safety, and quality. This is the reason why domestic organizations are challenged in context with better quality, fulfilling the emissions and safety standards, establishing the distribution and sales networks, and establishing after-sales maintenance networks and services effectively. Chinese manufactures can never develop the required brand image if they do not overcome these barriers against the foreign brands in international and domestic markets. The Chinese manufacturers must pay attention to these issues or they can never get rid of the image of being a negative country of image for improving their image within the domestic market and expanding within global markets (LIU, 2009).

Country of origin in Chinese consumer choice

There have been few studies that have studied the effect of country of origin on the choice of Chinese customers. The overall result showed that a product's country of origin is a significant consideration for the choice of Chinese customers in various product types. It was seen that the country of origin is a significant element in evaluating wine in a specific cue situation with the Chinese respondents likely to prefer imported or foreign brands to the domestic goods. The actual behavior of the respondents differed from their preference regarding Chinese grocery goods compared to the foreign goods. Country of origin was found to create a positive impact on the evaluation of the Chinese customers on milk powder produced in New Zealand (Zhao S. , 2012).

It also affected the rating of the respondents regarding the retail stores where the Shanghai respondents rated foreign stores better compared to the domestic stores whereas Chengdu respondents had rated the domestic stores in a more favorable manner compared to the foreign stores. It also affected the purchase decision of the Chinese respondents in around 9 product categories out of 12. It created a negative impact on the purchase decision of the Chinese respondents for goods made in Japan because of the way Japan treated China during Second World War. The Chinese producers passed off the domestic goods as West made so as to sell them from home. In 2009, the Indian government protested this act of the Chinese officials strongly regarding Chinese apparel, textile, and pharmaceutical manufacturers for putting 'Made in India' fake labels on the goods exported to the developing nations (Zhao S. , 2012).

As per study by Noble (2005) it seems that a product's country of origin is significant to the Chinese manufacturers and consumers alike in context with varied product categories. Chinese customers just like any other developing nation's customers perceive the goods imported from the developing nations to be of good quality compared to the domestic goods. Just like any other developing country, purchase and consumption of the costly imported goods in China shows greater material achievement helping in making an impression on others. The foreign manufactured goods have a symbolic value that explains their popularity in upcoming markets of Latin America, Eastern Europe, India, and China. It was anticipated in this study that the country of origin will turn out to be a significant consideration for automobile evaluations made by the Chinese consumers. It was also anticipated that the Chinese customers would evaluate the foreign automobiles in a favorable manner compared to the local brands. This would however result in reduced intentions for buying the local brands compared to the foreign brands (Noble, 2005).

Consumer Analysis

Wheel of Consumer Analysis, the consumer behavior model had been established by Jerry C. Olson and J. Paul Peter for defining people's car purchasing behaviors. As per the American Marketing Association, behavior of the consumers is defined as a dynamic interaction between cognition and affect, environmental events and behavior in such a way that people carry out their lives exchange aspects. Cognition/affect, behavior and environment are the three different aspects of the Wheel of Consumer Analysis that help the marketers in analyzing consumer behavior. Nevertheless, these factors influence and interact among each other making it difficult to separate any of the factors from each other. Marketers need to pay much attention to these elements for comprehending consumer behavior (Wright, 2006).

Both cognition and affect are significant in comprehending consumer behavior as cognition and affect indicate psychological and internal reactions, which customers might have as a response to the external environments objects like marketing stimuli or their personal behavior. In simple terms, cognition is all about thinking and affect is all about feelings.

Affective feelings can both be favorable and positive or unfavorable and negative. Whether negative or positive, they do play a role in affecting the consumer's decision. The best example for this is the Chinese consumer. Whenever a Chinese customer visits the car dealer for buying a car, they lay great stress on the service along with the behavior of the salesperson and the option packages. The most important factor for Chinese customers is the sincerity of the dealers while conducting business and not stress only on the cost. A number of international firms have idea that Chinese customers prefer negotiating in context with service and price (Tyagi, 2004).

Behavior

Behavior is the second significant factor affecting the customers. While cognition, affect deal with what a customer thinks, and feels, behavior is all about what the customer does. Consumer behavior example would be buying a product, visiting the store and watching a television commercial. A Chinese customer pays great attention to the information content rather than to entertainment features of any advertisement. There was a study, which showed that Chinese consumers were knowledgeable and sophisticated while making their purchase choices.

Environment

Environment is another factor referring to the social and physical features of the external world of the consumer on the micro and macro level. A macro environment comprises of general environmental characteristics like political system, economic conditions, demographics, and climate. A micro environment comprises of direct interactions between small groups of people like reference groups and families. Both these environments comprise of people, places, and objects that affect the recognition/affect and behavior of the customers. Friends in a Chinese community provide good reference specifically in context with durable and large goods purchases. Marketing strategies must adapt or change the physical and social environments to some extent (Zhao S. , 2012).

7. Research Method

The research study implements the quantitative research technique. Quantitative research is a way of conducting methodical empirical investigation for the social phenomenon with the help of statistical, mathematical, and computational methods. Such a type of research is all about developing as well as implementing the mathematical, theories and hypotheses models linked with this phenomenon. The process of measurement is quite significant for a quantitative research because it provides fundamental links between empirical observations and mathematical expressions of the quantitative associations. Quantitative data is always numerical in the form of statistics and percentage (Cooper & Schindler, 2006).

Research Design

The study conducts a survey of 100 respondents. The respondents were selected from public places, university campuses, apartment buildings, parks, workplaces, and shopping malls from the city of Haikou, Xiamen, Yinchuan, Lanzhou, Zhengzhou, Qingdao, Suzhou, Shenzhen, Shanghai, and Xi'an. Rural people had been excluded as they have different lifestyles and comparatively low income. Some questionnaires were delivered by email to the prospective respondents, which were self-administered.

The respondents will be made to evaluate the profiles of various automobiles that were developed with the help of conjoint analysis for studying the significance of country of origin in the eye of the Chinese customers while evaluating the automobiles. USA, China, Japan, and Germany were the country of origin that had been applied. USA, Japan, and Germany were chosen, as they were the dominating automobile manufacturers of the automobile market in China. The respondents will be asked to rank their profiles based on five key attributes that affect automobile purchase like country of origin, price, brand name, safety, and reliability (Saunders & Lewis, 2009).

8.   Research Limitation

This research study emphasizes on the growth of Chinese auto industry and its outstanding strategies to survive despite. Thus, the quantitative analysis will be limited only to the feedback given by the Taiwan customers. The key limitation of this study is only this. The study can be extended by stressing largely on the diversified areas and global cosmetic market with the help of direct marketing in context with this large platform.

References

- Amighini, A. (2012). The international expansion of Chinese auto firms: typology and trends. *International Journal of Automotive Technology & Management* , 33-90.

- Barbosa, F. (2010). Applying global trends: A look at China's auto industry. *McKinsey Quarterly* , 22-90.

- Batra, S. K. (2009). *Consumer Behaviour.* london: sage.

- Berkman, H. W. (1997). *Consumer behavior.* london: sage.

- Blythe, J. (2008). *Consumer Behaviour.* NEW YORK: CENAGE LEARNING .

- BUTNARU, C. (2009). SOCIAL PSYCHOLOGY AND MARKETING: THE CONSUMPTION GAME. UNDERSTANDING MARKETING AND CONSUMER BEHAVIOR THROUGH GAME THEORY. 22.

- Chiu, L. (2011). The Evolution of Supply Chain Management in Chinese Auto-Parts Manufacturers. *Business Dissertations.* , 88-90.

- Cooper, D. R., & Schindler, P. S. (2006). *Business Research Methods.* London: McGraw-Hill.

- Crowther, D., & Lancaster, G. (2012). *Research Methods.* London: Routledge.

- Evans, J. (2007). *CONSUMER BEHAVIOUR .* CHICAGO: ROUTLEDGE.

- Hawkins, D. I. (1998). *Consumer Behavior - Page 25.* london: cenage learniing.

- Kumar. (2005). *Research Methodology A Step-by-Step Guide For Beginners.* lONDON: Sage Publication.

- LIU, J. (2009). Corporate Governance and Technological Capability Development: Three Case Studies in the Chinese Auto Industry. . *Industry & Innovation.* , 33-90.

- Loudon. (2001). *Consumer Behavior 4/E.* london: sage.

- Miller, R. K. (2013). PART XIII: CONSUMER MARKETING: Chapter 87: DIRECT MARKETING. *Consumer Behavior;* , 90-189.

- Mo, T. (2011). CONSUMER BEHAVIOR IN GLOBAL MARKETS: DOES AMERICA RESHAPE CHINESE CONSUMERS' FLAVOR TOWARD LUXURY? . *AMA Summer Educators' Conference Proceedings* , 77-121.

- Noble, G. W. (2005). Executioner or Disciplinarian: WTO Accession and the Chinese Auto Industry. *Business & Politics.* , 22-90.

- Saunders, M. N., & Lewis, P. (2009). *Research Methods for Business Students.* London: Prentice Hall.

- Tyagi, C. L. (2004). *Consumer Behaviour.* LONDON: ROUTLEDGE.

- Warburton, M. (2008). Chinese Autos, Part 2: Can China Build a Competitive Car? A Unique Teardown Analysis. *Bernstein Global View - Chinese Autos* , 1-199.

- Weinberg, D. (2002). *Qualitative research methods* (1st ed.). Wiley-Blackwel.

- Wright, R. (2006). *Consumer behaviour.* Chicago: sage.

- Zhao, S. (2012). Changing employment relations in China: a comparative study of the auto and banking industries. . *International Journal of Human Resource Management.* , 22-90.

- Zhao, Z. (2009). Global Supply Chain and the Chinese Auto Industry. *Chinese Economy* , 3-90.